BRUSSELS & BRUGES
Christmas Market Winter Guide

2025-2026

Experience Belgium's Magical
Christmas Markets: Festive
Secrets ,Insider Tips, itineraries
&Unforgettable Winter Escapes"

Robert I. Manley

COPYRIGHT

TABLE OF CON

FORWARD

Whenever I think back to my first winter in Belgium, I can still see the glow of fairy lights reflected in the cobblestones, hear the laughter of children circling an ice rink, and smell the sweet mix of waffles and mulled wine drifting through the air. Stepping into Brussels and Bruges in December felt like stepping into a snow globe — everything was a little brighter, a little cozier, and far more magical than I could have imagined.

I wrote this guide because I know how it feels to crave that sense of wonder, to want a holiday that feels like a story you'll tell for years. Over the years, I've wandered these markets countless times — sometimes alone, sometimes with loved ones — and every visit left me with something new: a hidden stall with handcrafted lace, a quiet corner café serving the richest hot chocolate, or a breathtaking moment as Bruges' canals shimmered with light at dusk.

Travel, especially around the holidays, can feel overwhelming. Which market should you visit first? How do you avoid the crowds? Where do you stay when hotels book up quickly? I've been there — standing at train stations with too

many choices, wishing someone had told me the simplest way to plan it all. That's why this book exists: not just as a guide, but as a trusted companion.

Inside these pages, you'll find more than lists of attractions. I'll walk you through itineraries that feel like stories, introduce you to flavors you'll dream about long after you return home, and show you where to find authentic treasures that carry the spirit of Belgium back with you. Whether you're traveling as a couple, with children, with friends, or on your own, I want you to feel confident, prepared, and above all — excited.

Brussels and Bruges have a way of wrapping you in their warmth, even on the frostiest days. By the time you leave, you won't just have photographs and souvenirs; you'll carry with you the feeling of belonging to something timeless and beautiful.

So, take a deep breath, imagine the twinkle of a thousand lights, and let's begin this journey together.

INTRODUCTION

I still remember the first time I stepped off the train into a Belgian winter. The air was crisp, carrying the faint scent of roasted chestnuts, and the streets shimmered with fairy lights as if someone had draped the whole city in a velvet cloak of gold and silver. At that moment, I understood why people often say that winter in Belgium feels like stepping into a snow globe. Every cobblestoned alley glistens, every medieval façade glows, and every market square hums with laughter, music, and the warmth of shared traditions.

Winter here isn't just a season—it's an experience. It's a celebration of life lived in slow, delightful moments: warming your hands on a mug of velvety hot chocolate, hearing the jingle of carousel bells, or watching children skate in the shadow of towering Gothic spires. Belgium—especially Brussels and Bruges—transforms into a storybook come alive in wintertime, offering not only festive markets but also an atmosphere that wraps around you like the coziest of scarves.

In this chapter, let me take you by the hand and show you why these two cities shine so brightly in winter, what you should know before you go, and how to time your visit for maximum enchantment.

Why Brussels & Bruges Shine in Winter

Brussels and Bruges are like two siblings with distinct personalities, both dazzling in their own way during the holiday season.

Brussels, the capital, is grand and cosmopolitan, yet surprisingly intimate when dressed in winter's finery. The city's beating heart, the **Grand-Place**, becomes a stage for one of Europe's most magical winter spectacles: a breathtaking sound-and-light show that dances across ornate guildhalls and the towering Town Hall. Standing there, shoulder to shoulder with travelers from all over the world, you feel part of something bigger—an unspoken fellowship of awe. Add to that dozens of market stalls selling hand-crafted gifts, sizzling sausages, and spiced mulled wine, and Brussels transforms into a festive wonderland you'll want to get lost in.

Then there is **Bruges**, a jewel box of a city that seems built for fairy tales. Its canals mirror the glow of lanterns, and its medieval squares fill with chalets offering delicate lace, artisanal chocolates, and steaming waffles. Strolling through Bruges in winter feels like time travel—horses clip-clop past, bells chime from ancient towers, and the scent of warm speculoos biscuits drifts through the air. The **Market Square**, with its skating rink framed by candy-colored houses, is as charming as anything you'll see in Europe. If Brussels is about spectacle and scale, Bruges is about intimacy and timeless romance.

Together, the two cities embody the magic of Belgium in winter: Brussels for its vibrant energy and Bruges for its quiet enchantment. One offers the sparkle of a capital, the other the warmth of a medieval village. Both are unforgettable.

Quick Facts & Need-to-Know Essentials

Before you dive headfirst into the enchantment, here are some essentials that will help you navigate Belgium's winter with ease:

- **Languages Spoken:** Belgium has three official languages—French, Dutch (often referred to as Flemish in

Flanders), and German. In Brussels, you'll hear both French and Dutch, while Bruges leans heavily on Dutch. Don't worry, though—English is widely spoken, especially in the tourist areas.

- **Currency:** The Euro (€). Credit cards are generally accepted, but having some cash on hand is wise, especially at smaller stalls in the markets.
- **Weather:** Expect cold, often hovering between 0°C and 6°C (32°F to 43°F). Snow isn't guaranteed, but when it does fall, it adds a magical dusting over rooftops and squares. Rain is more common, so pack a warm, waterproof coat, gloves, and sturdy shoes for cobblestones that can get slippery.
- **Getting Around:** Belgium is blessed with one of Europe's most efficient rail systems. Trains between Brussels and Bruges run frequently and take just over an hour, making it easy to explore both cities in a single trip. Within cities, walking is the best way to soak in the atmosphere, though trams and buses are available.
- **Food & Drink Highlights:** Belgian hot chocolate is legendary, waffles are irresistible, and mulled wine will keep

you warm in the chill. Don't skip trying *stoofvlees* (a rich Flemish beef stew) or a cone of crispy Belgian fries with mayo. And of course, Belgian beer is an experience in itself.

- **Etiquette Tip:** A polite "Bonjour" or "Goedendag" goes a long way with market vendors. Smile, try a greeting in the local language, and you'll be met with warmth.

Armed with these basics, you'll move through Brussels and Bruges with ease, free to immerse yourself fully in the joy and charm of the season.

Market Season at a Glance

Timing is everything when it comes to catching the full glow of Belgium's Christmas markets.

- **Brussels:** The city's famed **Winter Wonders festival** usually runs from late November through the first week of January. Highlights include the Grand-Place light show, the giant Christmas tree, and over 200 stalls stretching from the Bourse to Place Sainte-Catherine. If you want to feel the energy of a bustling European capital at its most festive, this is your spot.

- **Bruges:** Slightly smaller but dripping with charm, Bruges' markets typically open around the same time—late November—and run until early January. The main market square becomes the city's glowing heart, with a skating rink and stalls offering everything from lace ornaments to artisan cheeses. Bruges' slower pace means you can linger longer at stalls, chat with locals, and savor the details.

- **Best Time to Visit:** Early December is magical, with fewer crowds and the markets in full swing. However, the weeks just before Christmas bring a special electricity to the air, when both cities are at their most dazzling. If you prefer a quieter experience, consider visiting just after Christmas, when festivities continue but the rush has eased.

Whether you begin in Brussels or Bruges, plan to experience both if you can. Their markets complement each other beautifully, offering a blend of grandeur and intimacy. A weekend in each city feels like two chapters of the same fairy tale.

Stepping into the Snow Globe

As I reflect on winters spent wandering through Belgium's cobblestoned streets, I can tell you this: these markets are more than events. They are living, breathing traditions that invite you to slow down, to savor, to connect—with strangers over steaming mugs, with artisans through their handmade crafts, and with the spirit of the season itself.

So as you step into Belgium this winter, prepare to be enchanted. Allow yourself to be swept away by the glow of lights, the aromas of festive treats, and the timeless charm of Brussels and Bruges. In the chapters ahead, I'll guide you through every sparkling square, hidden alley, and cozy café, but for now, let's pause together in this snow globe moment, where winter truly feels like magic.

PLANNING YOUR PERFECT WINTER ESCAPE

When it comes to winter travel, I've learned one golden truth: the magic happens when preparation meets spontaneity. Brussels and Bruges are undeniably enchanting during the festive season, but like any popular destination, the difference between a stressful trip and a seamless, joy-filled adventure lies in the planning. Don't worry—I'll walk you through everything step by step, so instead of fretting about logistics, you'll be free to soak in the glow of fairy lights, sip hot chocolate, and let yourself get swept up in the festive spirit.

Think of this chapter as your toolkit. Together, we'll pin down the best dates, get smart about crowds, pack the right gear, and tackle flights, hotels, and experiences with confidence. We'll even talk about travel insurance—a topic that may not sparkle like a Christmas tree but can save you from serious headaches. My aim is simple: by the time you finish this section, you'll feel fully prepared, calm, and excited to step into Belgium's winter wonderland.

Best Dates to Visit & How to Avoid the Crowds

One of the first questions I always get is: *When should I go?* The short answer is: there isn't a bad time to visit during the market season. But if you want to balance the atmosphere with comfort, timing matters.

- **Late November to Early December:** The markets usually kick off in the last week of November. Visiting in those first two weeks of December can be a dream. Everything is in full swing, the decorations sparkle, and yet the crowds haven't reached their pre-Christmas frenzy. Hotel prices tend to be slightly lower too.
- **Mid to Late December (Christmas Week):** This is peak season. The markets are buzzing, children are out of school, and the atmosphere is electric. If you thrive on the energy of bustling squares and don't mind weaving through crowds, this is when the cities are at their most magical. Just book well in advance.
- **Between Christmas & New Year's:** A slightly calmer period. The markets stay open, the decorations remain, but

the crowds thin a little as many visitors return home. If you're hoping for a more relaxed experience, this is a sweet spot.

- **Early January (Final Days):** The markets usually wind down by the first week of January. While there's a quiet, reflective charm to the last days, some stalls may start closing early, and the energy is softer. This is perfect if you're looking for a more subdued, contemplative winter trip.

Avoiding the Crowds:

- Go early in the day. Markets tend to be quieter in the mornings and early afternoons, especially on weekdays.
- Visit smaller squares first. In Brussels, the Grand-Place draws the biggest crowds, but areas like Place Sainte-Catherine and the Bourse markets are lively without being overwhelming.
- In Bruges, linger down side streets or at stalls off the main square to find breathing space.

My personal strategy? Arrive midweek in early December, stay through a weekend, and you'll get the best of both worlds: calm moments plus the buzz of peak festivities.

Weather, Packing & Dressing Warm

Belgium in winter has a distinct personality—sometimes moody, sometimes glittering, always chilly. The weather rarely drops into bitter cold like Scandinavia, but it can be damp, and that dampness seeps into your bones if you're not dressed properly. Let's make sure you're cozy and comfortable so the weather never gets in the way of your enjoyment.

What to Expect:

- Temperatures hover between 0°C and 6°C (32°F to 43°F).
- Snow is possible, but not common. More likely you'll encounter drizzle or grey skies. Don't be discouraged—those moody skies make the Christmas lights even more enchanting.

Packing Tips:

1. **Layer Smartly:** Think base layer (thermal top), mid-layer (sweater or

fleece), and outer layer (a warm, waterproof coat). Layers allow you to adapt when you step indoors into heated cafés.

2. **Waterproof Essentials:** A good coat with a hood, waterproof boots with traction, and an umbrella that won't fold inside-out in the wind. Belgian cobblestones can get slippery.

3. **Accessories Matter:** Gloves, a scarf, and a hat are not optional—they're your best friends. I always pack two sets in case one gets wet.

4. **Footwear:** Comfortable boots with thick soles. You'll walk a lot, and style is pointless if your toes are frozen.

5. **Day Bag:** A small backpack or crossbody to hold your umbrella, camera, water bottle, and market finds.

I've made the mistake once of underestimating Belgian drizzle. After an hour of damp feet, the magic dimmed quickly. Since then, waterproof boots are my non-negotiable. Dress wisely, and the weather won't just be bearable—it'll feel part of the adventure.

Booking Flights, Hotels & Experiences in Advance

Now, let's talk logistics. Planning ahead doesn't just save you stress; it unlocks the best choices and often the best deals.

Flights:

- Brussels Airport (Zaventem) is the main international hub, but don't overlook Charleroi if you're flying budget airlines within Europe.
- Book at least three months in advance if you're traveling in December—fares rise quickly as Christmas approaches.
- Flexibility helps. Flying midweek (Tuesday or Wednesday) often saves money and avoids crowded flights.

Hotels:

- In Brussels, aim for areas near the Grand-Place, Sainte-Catherine, or Dansaert for easy access to the markets.
- In Bruges, staying in the historic center means everything is walkable. Book early—Bruges has fewer rooms than Brussels, and they fill fast in December.

- Consider boutique hotels or charming B&Bs over large chains—they often feel more in tune with the festive spirit.
- If you're splitting time between both cities, don't overcomplicate things. Two nights in Brussels, two in Bruges is a solid plan for a short trip.

Experiences:

- Reserve guided tours in advance—like chocolate-making workshops, beer tastings, or canal boat rides in Bruges. They often sell out around Christmas.
- If you want a special dining experience (such as dinner in Bruges' Markt Square overlooking the skating rink), book weeks ahead.
- Brussels' Winter Wonders also includes a Ferris wheel, ice rink, and light shows—buying tickets online beforehand can save you queues.

My philosophy is simple: the more you book in advance, the more freedom you'll have on the ground. Imagine arriving with flights, hotels, and key experiences locked in—suddenly, your mind is free to wander and enjoy.

Travel Insurance & Peace-of-Mind Tips

Here's where I put on my seasoned-traveler hat and give you advice that's less glamorous but absolutely essential. Travel insurance may not sparkle like Bruges' Christmas lights, but it's the safety net that lets you enjoy your trip without nagging worries.

Why You Need It:

- Winter weather can disrupt flights. Insurance ensures you're covered if you face cancellations or delays.
- Crowded events increase the risk of small mishaps—losing your bag, misplacing your passport, or slipping on icy cobblestones.
- Medical care in Belgium is excellent, but without insurance, costs can pile up quickly for non-EU visitors.

What to Look For:

1. **Medical Coverage:** Make sure it covers emergencies, hospital stays, and repatriation.

2. **Trip Cancellation/Interruption:** Protects you if illness, family emergencies, or unforeseen events keep you from traveling.
3. **Lost or Stolen Belongings:** Handy when you're navigating busy markets.
4. **Winter-Specific Coverage:** Some policies even cover delayed luggage or missed connections due to weather.

Peace-of-Mind Tips:

- Keep both a digital and paper copy of your insurance policy and emergency contact numbers.
- Save digital copies of your passport and travel documents in your email or cloud storage.
- Share your itinerary with a trusted friend or family member back home.
- Carry a small first-aid kit (plasters, painkillers, motion sickness tablets). You'll be glad you have it when shops are closed on a Sunday.

Knowing you're covered creates a mental shift. You stop worrying about what *might* go wrong and start savoring what's going *so right*.

Bringing It All Together

Planning your Belgian winter escape is a little like preparing a festive feast: it takes a bit of organization, but the rewards are delicious. By choosing your dates wisely, dressing for the weather, booking the essentials, and safeguarding yourself with insurance, you'll give yourself the gift of peace of mind.

When you arrive in Brussels or Bruges and see the twinkle of the first market lights, you won't be distracted by "what ifs" or scrambling for last-minute bookings. Instead, you'll be free to live fully in the moment—whether that's skating under Bruges' belfry, sipping mulled wine in Brussels, or wandering through cobblestone alleys dusted with frost.

Trust me: put in the preparation now, and the rest of your journey will unfold like the most beautiful storybook.

GETTING THERE & AROUND

One of the things I love about Belgium—besides the chocolate, of course—is just how easy it is to get around. The country may be small, but that's part of its charm: everything feels close, connected, and accessible. Whether you're arriving from overseas or hopping over from another European city, Belgium's transport system makes exploring Brussels and Bruges a breeze. Let me walk you through the best ways to arrive, move between the two cities, and navigate once you're on the ground.

Flying into Belgium: Airports & Transfers

If you're flying in from abroad, chances are you'll land at **Brussels Airport (Zaventem)**, the main international hub. Located just 12 kilometers (about 7 miles) northeast of the city center, it's incredibly well-connected. I usually recommend taking the train straight from the airport into Brussels Central Station—it's quick (around 20 minutes), comfortable, and much less hassle than a taxi in traffic. Trains run every 10 minutes during peak times, so you're never waiting long.

There's also **Brussels South Charleroi Airport**, often used by low-cost airlines like Ryanair. Don't be fooled by the name—it's about an hour south of Brussels. Transfers are easy, though: shuttle buses run directly from Charleroi to Brussels Midi Station, and from there you can connect to the rest of the city or hop on a train to Bruges. It's not as convenient as Zaventem, but if you're chasing budget fares, it can be worth the detour.

If your main destination is Bruges, don't worry—you don't need a separate airport. Flying into Brussels and taking the train to Bruges is the simplest and fastest route.

Trains & Eurostar Options from Europe & the UK

Belgium really shines when it comes to trains. If you're already in Europe, you might not even need to fly.

From **Paris**, the high-speed **Thalys** train gets you to Brussels in about 1 hour 30 minutes. From **Amsterdam**, it's about 2 hours. And from **London**, the **Eurostar** is one of my favorite ways to arrive: you board at St. Pancras, zip under the Channel, and step off in Brussels Midi in just over 2 hours. It's stress-free, scenic, and you skip the airport queues entirely.

What I love about these train options is how central they leave you. No transfers, no long taxi rides—you're already in the heart of Belgium. Tickets are cheapest if booked in advance (sometimes months ahead), especially on popular routes like Eurostar during December.

If you're arriving from elsewhere in Belgium or neighboring Germany, regular intercity trains are straightforward and reliable. Belgium's rail network is compact, and delays are rare enough that I always recommend trains over renting a car.

Brussels ↔ Bruges Day Trips Made Easy

Now let's talk about one of the joys of Belgian travel: how ridiculously easy it is to hop between Brussels and Bruges.

The two cities are just over an hour apart by train, and services run roughly every 20–30 minutes throughout the day. Trains leave from **Brussels Central**, **Midi**, and **Nord** stations, and arrive directly at **Bruges Station**, which is about a 10-minute walk (or a short bus ride) from the historic center.

Here's what makes it stress-free:

- **No reservations needed.** Just buy a ticket at the station or online. Trains don't sell out.
- **Flat fares.** A standard ticket costs the same whether you book weeks ahead or on the day.
- **Scenic ride.** The route takes you through gentle countryside dotted with villages—an easy, relaxing start to your day.

I often suggest basing yourself in Brussels and doing a day trip to Bruges if your time is tight. On the flip side, if you're staying in Bruges, a quick train into Brussels gives you the capital's festive buzz without the hassle of changing hotels. Either way, you can comfortably explore both cities in one trip.

Navigating Local Transport & Walking Routes

Once you're in the city, you'll find Brussels and Bruges refreshingly walkable. In fact, walking is often the best way to soak up the atmosphere. Cobblestone lanes, hidden courtyards, little cafés tucked between medieval façades—you'd miss all that if you rushed around on buses.

In Brussels:

- The main Christmas markets and Winter Wonders attractions are clustered in the center: Grand-Place, Bourse, Place Sainte-Catherine. You can walk between them in under 15 minutes.
- If you do need transport, the metro, trams, and buses are reliable. A single ticket covers all modes, and you can buy passes at stations or via apps. The STIB network is well signposted and easy to follow.
- Taxis and ride-shares are available but often unnecessary unless you're carrying heavy bags.

In Bruges:

- Bruges' charm lies in wandering on foot. The historic center is compact—you can cross it in 20 minutes. Walking lets you linger on bridges, pause to admire canal reflections, or stop for an impromptu hot chocolate.
- From the train station, you can either walk 10–15 minutes into the Market Square or hop on a local bus if your luggage is heavy.
- Bikes are also popular, even in winter. Locals cycle everywhere, and you'll find rental shops near the station. Just be cautious on cobblestones if it's rainy or icy.

Walking Routes I Love:

- In Brussels, start at the Grand-Place, then wander toward Place Sainte-Catherine via Rue de la Bourse—it's like walking through a corridor of festive lights.
- In Bruges, leave the main square behind and stroll along the canals near Rozenhoedkaai. In winter, the reflections of fairy lights on the water look like something from a painting.

Both cities reward slow exploration, so don't plan to rush from A to B. The beauty lies in the detours: a chocolatier's window, a caroller's song, a hidden courtyard glowing with lanterns.

Final word on Getting Around

Traveling in Belgium is wonderfully straightforward. Whether you're flying into Brussels, zipping in on a Eurostar, or hopping on a local train, the connections are smooth and stress-free. Once you're here, walking between markets and sights feels natural, and the compact size of both Brussels and Bruges means you'll spend less time in transit and more time savoring the festive atmosphere.

Think of Belgium as a gift that's easy to unwrap. The logistics are simple, leaving you free to focus on what really matters: the warm mulled wine, the sparkle of lights, and the joy of experiencing winter magic at your own pace.

BRUSSELS WINTER WONDERS

Every December, Brussels pulls off something remarkable. The entire city center transforms into a grand stage for **Winter Wonders**—a month-long festival of markets, lights, music, food, and pure seasonal joy. It's not just a Christmas market; it's a sprawling celebration that fills the city with warmth and sparkle, even on the chilliest winter nights.

I'll never forget the first time I stepped into the Grand-Place during Winter Wonders. My breath caught—not from the cold, but from the sight of golden lights rippling across the Gothic façades while carols swelled around me. The crowd gasped together, strangers huddled close, all eyes lifted in awe. At that moment, I realized: this is more than sightseeing; this is experiencing the heartbeat of Brussels at its most magical.

Let me take you on a journey through this dazzling event—zone by zone, bite by bite—so when you arrive, you'll feel like you're rediscovering a place you already know and love.

Market Layout & Must-See Zones

Winter Wonders isn't confined to a single square. Instead, it stretches across the historic heart of Brussels, weaving together markets, rides, performances, and festive décor. The layout feels like following a trail of twinkling lights that beckons you deeper and deeper into the celebration.

Here's how I like to think of it:

- **The Grand-Place:** The jewel of the festival. The centerpiece here is the light-and-sound show, but don't rush through. During the day, the square hosts the giant Christmas tree and a beautiful nativity scene, perfect for a quiet moment of reflection before the evening crowds gather.
- **Bourse (Stock Exchange) Area:** Just a short stroll from the Grand-Place, this zone brims with stalls. The scents of sizzling sausages and mulled wine hit you first, followed by the colorful displays of ornaments, scarves, and Belgian lace. It's lively, bustling, and perfect for picking up gifts.

- **Place Sainte-Catherine:** This is the true heart of Winter Wonders' market stalls. Picture rows of wooden chalets, each glowing warmly against the winter night, selling everything from hand-carved wooden toys to artisanal cheese. Here you'll also find the big Ferris wheel—the "Grande Roue"—illuminated in shifting colors and offering panoramic views of Brussels dressed in holiday finery.
- **Marché aux Poissons (Fish Market):** Despite the name, you won't find seafood here during Winter Wonders. Instead, it's a haven of food stalls—cheese, waffles, beer, chocolate. This is where the aromas really grab hold of you, pulling you from one treat to the next.
- **Other Corners & Connections:** As you wander, you'll stumble across carousels with whimsical wooden animals, street performers juggling or playing festive tunes, and little surprises tucked into alleys. That's the beauty of Brussels: Winter Wonders spills into the fabric of the city, so every corner feels alive.

The whole market is walkable in the evening, but don't rush. Take your time to soak in each square's personality—each one adds a new layer to the festive story.

The Grand-Place Light & Sound Show

If Winter Wonders has a crown jewel, it's the **Grand-Place light-and-sound show**. No matter how many times I've seen it, it still sends shivers down my spine.

Picture this: the square goes quiet, the crowd gathers shoulder to shoulder, and suddenly music swells—carols, classical pieces, sometimes even modern festive beats. Then the buildings themselves come alive. Lights ripple across the 17th-century guildhalls, the Town Hall spire glows, and patterns dance across the ornate façades as though the architecture itself is performing.

The best part? It happens several times each evening, usually on the hour, and it's free. You don't need a ticket; just find a spot in the square and look up. For me, the magic is in the shared awe. People of every age and nationality stand together in wonder, cameras raised, children perched on shoulders, everyone wrapped in scarves and smiles.

My tip: arrive 10–15 minutes early if you want a good view in the center. But honestly, anywhere you stand, the effect is mesmerizing. One evening, I stood in a corner of the square with a cone of fries in hand, and even from that angle, the light seemed to wash over me like a tide of gold.

It's hard to describe the feeling fully—it's not just about the visuals but the atmosphere. It feels like Brussels itself is singing.

Top Stalls, Crafts & Seasonal Gifts

Now, let's talk about shopping. Winter Wonders is a treasure trove of stalls—over 200 of them—selling everything from holiday décor to gourmet treats. Wandering the chalets feels like flipping through a catalog of Belgium's creativity and craftsmanship.

Crafts & Gifts to Look For:

- **Handmade Ornaments:** Delicate glass baubles, wooden stars, and lace decorations that feel authentically Belgian.

- **Knitted Scarves & Gloves:** Perfect for keeping warm as you wander, and often made by local artisans.
- **Belgian Lace:** Bruges may be more famous for lace, but you'll still find intricate lace pieces here—doilies, coasters, even tiny lace angels.
- **Wooden Toys:** Classic, old-world toys that make meaningful gifts for children (or nostalgic adults).
- **Candles & Soaps:** Many stalls offer handmade candles scented with cinnamon, pine, or vanilla—aromas that feel like winter in a jar.

I love browsing slowly, chatting with vendors, and hearing their stories. Buying from these stalls feels personal; you're not just purchasing a gift, you're supporting a craft handed down through generations.

Belgian Treats to Taste at the Market

If you only remember one thing from this chapter, let it be this: **come hungry**. Winter Wonders is a feast for all senses, but especially your taste buds.

What to Eat & Drink:

- **Waffles:** Brussels waffles are lighter, crispier, and usually rectangular. Eat them plain with a dusting of sugar, or pile them with cream, strawberries, and chocolate sauce. Standing in the cold with a warm waffle in hand is pure joy.
- **Speculoos Biscuits:** Spiced shortbread cookies that taste like cinnamon and caramelized sugar. Dip them into hot chocolate for a true Belgian experience.
- **Frites (Fries):** Served in a paper cone with mayonnaise or sauce and eaten standing up as steam curls into the night air.
- **Stoofvlees:** A rich Flemish beef stew, slow-cooked in beer until tender. Served with fries, it's hearty and warming.
- **Hot Chocolate:** Thick, creamy, and often made with real Belgian chocolate melted into milk. Many stalls let you choose your chocolate—dark, milk, or white.
- **Mulled Wine (Vin Chaud/Glühwein):** Spiced, steaming, and served in festive mugs. Perfect for warming your hands.

- **Belgian Beer:** Winter ales with hints of spice and caramel are especially festive. Look for limited-edition brews crafted just for the holiday season.

My personal ritual? Start with mulled wine, nibble a speculoos biscuit, then dive into a cone of fries. Once I've warmed up, I finish with hot chocolate and a waffle. It's indulgent, yes, but if you can't indulge here, where can you?

Family-Friendly Fun: Ice Rink, Santa's Grotto & More

Winter Wonders isn't just for shoppers or foodies—it's a playground for families too.

- **Ice Rink:** Located near Place de la Monnaie or Place Sainte-Catherine (locations can change slightly year to year), the rink glows with lights while skaters glide to festive tunes. Even if you don't skate, it's delightful to watch families laugh and wobble across the ice.
- **Ferris Wheel:** The "Grande Roue" towers over Place Sainte-Catherine, offering views of the city's rooftops, glowing markets, and the illuminated cathedral spires. At night, it feels like floating above a sea of twinkling stars.

- **Carousels:** Brussels' carousels are whimsical works of art, with wooden sea creatures, airships, and fantastical animals replacing traditional horses. Kids adore them, but I've seen plenty of adults riding too.
- **Santa's Grotto:** A cozy chalet where little ones can meet Santa, pose for photos, and share their wish lists. It's sweet, charming, and gives parents a chance to rest with mulled wine in hand.

The beauty of Winter Wonders is that it offers something for everyone. Children can ride carousels, teens can skate or snack on waffles, and adults can sip beer or browse stalls. It's multigenerational joy in its purest form.

Final Word

Walking through Brussels during Winter Wonders feels like moving through a living storybook. Lights shimmer off cobblestones, laughter drifts through the air, and every corner offers another surprise. Whether you're marveling at the Grand-Place light show, sipping steaming hot chocolate, or spinning on a carousel, the experience is more than the sum of its parts—it's a celebration of life, community, and joy.

I always tell friends: don't think of Winter Wonders as just a market. Think of it as the heartbeat of Brussels in December, where traditions meet modern creativity and where strangers become companions in wonder. By the time you leave, with arms full of gifts and a belly full of waffles, you'll feel not just like you've visited Belgium, but like you've been part of something truly magical.

So bundle up, follow the glow of the lights, and let Brussels sweep you into its winter embrace.

BRUGES WINTER GLOW

If Brussels dazzles with spectacle and scale, Bruges seduces with intimacy and warmth. I've always felt that if ever there were a town designed to be seen in winter, it is Bruges. The cobblestones glisten with frost, canals shimmer like liquid silver beneath bridges draped in fairy lights, and the air hums softly with bells and carols. There's a dreamlike quality here, a sense that you've slipped through time into a storybook. Bruges doesn't overwhelm—it embraces you, draws you into its quiet, glowing magic.

Markt Square & Simon Stevinplein Highlights

My first stop is always **Markt Square**, the beating heart of Bruges, where the Winter Glow festivities bloom each year. The square, surrounded by gabled guild houses painted in bold reds, greens, and ochres, is transformed into a glowing stage. Strings of golden lights connect rooftop to rooftop, like stars stitched into a net above the square. In the center, a towering Christmas tree rises proudly, shimmering with ornaments that seem to reflect every joyful face gazing up at them.

Wander among the wooden chalets scattered across the square and you'll feel that irresistible pull of holiday magic. Each stall is a miniature treasure chest—one spilling over with woolen scarves hand-knitted in earthy tones, another gleaming with glass baubles catching the light like tiny frozen rainbows. Some vendors smile behind steaming vats of glühwein, ladling mulled wine into cups that warm your fingers before they even touch your lips.

A few streets away, **Simon Stevinplein** is quieter but no less enchanting. The square here feels more intimate, with market huts huddled under trees strung with twinkling lights. I've always loved this corner—it's where you find the little details that make Bruges so special. Artisans here are often locals, and I've come across lace-makers showing delicate patterns worked with nimble fingers, or chocolatiers selling truffles infused with flavors you'll never find in tourist-heavy shops. If Markt is the main stage, Simon Stevinplein is the whispered secret: softer, subtler, but just as memorable.

Ice Rink, Light Festival & Canal Magic

Every winter, Bruges reinvents its magic with a mix of tradition and innovation, and nowhere is this more evident than in its **ice rink** and **light installations**. The ice rink, often set at the heart of Market Square or nearby Burg Square depending on the year's layout, is the kind that makes you forget time. Couples glide hand in hand, children wobble and laugh, and there's always someone spinning gracefully while the rest of us cling to the edge, grinning through the cold. The sound of blades scratching ice, mixed with carols echoing through the square, feels like the soundtrack of winter itself.

Then there's the **Light Experience Trail**, a fairly recent addition to Bruges' Winter Glow, and one that's become a favorite of mine. Imagine walking through historic streets illuminated not just by fairy lights but by modern, artistic light installations designed to highlight the city's medieval beauty in fresh ways. One moment you're standing beneath an archway bathed in ethereal blue light, the next you're crossing a bridge where twinkling orbs seem to float above the canal. It's not just festive—it's magical storytelling with light.

And speaking of canals, Bruges' waterways are pure enchantment in winter. Even without a boat ride, the simple act of strolling along Rozenhoedkaai at dusk is unforgettable. The view—medieval rooftops mirrored in the still, dark water, with lanterns glowing from windows—looks like it's been lifted straight from a painting. On evenings when mist drifts in, the canals blur into something dreamlike, a scene you'll carry in your memory long after the trip.

Shopping for Lace, Chocolate & Artisanal Souvenirs

It wouldn't be Bruges without its artisans, and winter seems to make their creations feel even more precious.

Lace is perhaps Bruges' most famous craft. Stepping into a lace shop here feels like stepping into a gallery of patience and tradition. Handmade lace, with its intricate patterns, makes for a delicate but lasting souvenir. I remember watching an elderly woman demonstrate bobbin lace once—her fingers moving so quickly, yet with such grace, that it felt like watching someone weave snowflakes.

Then there's **chocolate**. Oh, the chocolate. Every street seems to exhale the scent of cocoa, and inside shops, the displays are irresistible. Truffles dusted with cocoa powder, pralines filled with caramel or hazelnut, chocolate bars infused with spices or orange peel—each bite feels like a love letter to winter. I always buy a small box to take home, though it rarely survives the journey.

Beyond the classics, Bruges' markets also brim with **artisanal souvenirs**. Hand-carved wooden toys, beeswax candles, local cheeses wrapped in rustic paper—all feel more authentic than mass-produced trinkets. What I especially love is that many of these items carry the story of the maker. When you speak with the artisans themselves, their pride in their craft makes the purchase feel personal, meaningful, and connected to the soul of Bruges.

Evening Atmosphere: Bruges by Candlelight

If there's one moment that defines Bruges in winter for me, it's the evening. As day fades and the last shoppers head home, the town exhales into something softer, more romantic. Candles flicker in café windows, lanterns glow along winding streets, and the hush of footsteps on cobblestones becomes the rhythm of the night.

I love to wander after dark, letting instinct guide me rather than a map. I might end up in Burg Square, where the City Hall's Gothic façade glows golden against the night sky, or tucked into a side street where a family-run tavern beckons with laughter and the promise of hot chocolate topped with cream.

Bruges at night feel both intimate and infinite. There's nostalgia in the air, as though every corner holds the echo of centuries gone by. Yet there's also something timeless—the sense that whether you're a traveler in 2025 or 1525, the glow of candlelight on the canals would stir the same wonder.

If you're lucky enough to be here with someone special, Bruges is endlessly romantic. Share a hot mulled cider, take a moonlit stroll along Minnewater (aptly named the "Lake of Love"), and you'll feel as though the town itself is conspiring to make your visit unforgettable.

Final Word

Bruges doesn't clamor for your attention—it whispers to you, and in those whispers, it creates memories you'll cherish forever. It's not the biggest market in Europe, nor the loudest. But it doesn't need to be. Its beauty lies in the details: the frost on a lace windowpane, the soft chords of a violinist playing in the square, the way chocolate melts slowly on your tongue as you wander through ancient streets.

For me, Bruges is the definition of winter romance. It's a place that feels untouched by time, a town that glows from within, offering not just a festive celebration but a moment of stillness, wonder, and connection. And when you leave, you'll carry its glow with you—like a candle that never quite goes out.

WHERE TO STAY — HOTELS, HOSTELS & HIDEAWAYS

Finding the right place to stay is one of those details that can make or break your winter escape. I've learned over the years that the best accommodation isn't always about star ratings—it's about how it supports your experience. Do you want to step out your door into the glow of twinkling lights? Do you prefer a quieter retreat to return to after the bustle of the market? Or maybe you want to balance comfort with budget so you can spend more on mulled wine and gifts. Let me guide you through Brussels and Bruges with options for every style of traveler.

Best Neighborhoods in Brussels

Brussels is a bigger, busier city than Bruges, so where you stay can really shape your experience.

- **City Centre (Grand-Place & Sainte-Catherine):** If your priority is being at the heart of the Winter Wonders market, this is the spot. You'll be steps from the Grand-Place, with its dazzling light show, and surrounded by market chalets, restaurants, and shops. The energy is infectious, but it does mean higher prices and more noise. Perfect if you love being in the middle of the action.

- **Sablon & Louise Districts:** A little removed from the market frenzy, these areas offer boutique hotels, antique shops, and a slightly more refined atmosphere. You'll find beautiful cafés and chocolatiers, and it's still only a 15–20 day walk or quick tram ride into the market zones.

- **European Quarter:** This neighborhood is quieter at night (many offices here), and hotels can sometimes be more affordable during the winter weekends. It's less atmospheric but practical if you prefer modern comfort over festive hustle.

I personally love staying near Sainte-Catherine—it feels like the market is your backyard, and you can always retreat to a side street café when you need a breather.

Best Neighborhoods in Bruges

Bruges is more compact, so you can't really go wrong—but subtle differences matter.

- **Historic Centre (Markt & Burg Squares):** Staying right in the medieval heart means you wake up to the sound of bells and step into the market within minutes. It's wonderfully romantic but can come with a premium price.
- **Canal Districts:** Tucked just beyond the main squares, these neighborhoods offer charming guesthouses overlooking tranquil waterways. They feel quieter, more intimate, and still only a 10-minute walk to the markets. Ideal if you want fairy-tale charm without crowds at your doorstep.
- **Near the Train Station:** More practical than picturesque, but if you're coming for just a night or two and plan day trips, staying near the station can save time. Hotels here are often more modern and budget-friendly.

For me, the Canal Districts strike the perfect balance—close enough to the magic, yet peaceful when you want to slip away.

Accommodation by Budget

Every traveler's budget is different, and the good news is that both Brussels and Bruges offer plenty of choice.

- **Luxury:**

    - In **Brussels**, look at places like Rocco Forte's Hotel Amigo near the Grand-Place or Sofitel Le Louise for chic comfort.
    - In **Bruges**, the Relais Bourgondisch Cruyce is unforgettable, perched right on the canals with old-world elegance that feels like stepping into a painting. These stays are indulgent but transform the trip into something extraordinary.

- **Mid-Range:**

    - Brussels has plenty of boutique hotels near Sainte-Catherine or the Sablon, giving you character without breaking the bank.
    - In Bruges, guesthouses and family-run B&Bs offer cozy rooms, hearty breakfasts, and

personal touches that often outshine larger hotels.

- **Budget-Friendly:**

    ○ Hostels like Sleep Well in Brussels or Snuffel Hostel in Bruges are clean, central, and surprisingly stylish. They're not just for backpackers—you'll meet fellow travelers, which can be part of the fun.
    ○ Budget hotels near Brussels Midi or Bruges station are also good options if you're mainly looking for a clean bed and a place to stash your bags.

I've found that in winter, even budget stays feel special—because the magic of the markets is always just outside your door.

Booking Tips for Peak Market Weekends

Winter market season in Belgium is hugely popular, so a little planning goes a long way. Here's what I've learned (sometimes the hard way):

- **Book Early:** For peak weekends in December, especially around St. Nicholas (early December) and Christmas itself, hotels can sell out months in advance. The earlier you secure your room, the more options you'll have.
- **Flexibility Helps:** If your schedule allows, consider visiting on weekdays. Hotels are less crowded, rates are often lower, and the markets feel more relaxed.
- **Check Cancellation Policies:** Weather, strikes, or personal plans can change. I always opt for flexible bookings where possible, even if it costs a little more. Peace of mind is worth it.
- **Think About Transport Links:** If you're splitting time between Brussels and Bruges, being near a train station (without sacrificing too much charm) can save you hassle. For example, staying near Brussels Midi makes Eurostar connections easy, while Bruges' small station is a quick walk from the center.
- **Consider Extras:** Some hotels offer seasonal packages that include things like mulled wine on arrival, breakfast

hampers, or tickets to local events. These little touches can elevate your stay and add value.

Final Word

The beauty of traveling to Brussels and Bruges in winter is that there's no single "right" choice. Whether you're tucked into a grand hotel by the Grand-Place, sharing stories with new friends in a hostel lounge, or curled up by a canal-side fireplace in Bruges, you'll find that the magic of the season seeps into your stay.

I've stayed in all sorts of places here—luxury suites, humble guesthouses, modern hostels—and each has shaped my experience in a unique way. What matters most is matching your accommodation to your travel style. Do you want convenience, quiet, romance, or budget-friendliness? Once you know that, the perfect place will find you.

And remember, the true magic isn't just in the room you book—it's in the glow of the markets, the laughter in the streets, and the way these cities embrace you during the winter season. Wherever you lay your head, Brussels and Bruges will feel like home.

FOOD & DRINK ADVENTURES

If there's one thing Belgium does spectacularly well—beyond fairy-tale squares and glittering markets—it's food. Every visit here feels like a culinary adventure, and I've never left without loosening my belt a little. Between sizzling market stalls, indulgent sweet treats, world-famous beer, and cafés tucked into cobbled lanes, Brussels and Bruges offer flavors that warm you from the inside out. Let me take you through the tastes, textures, and aromas I never miss when I'm here.

Market Street Food Must-Trys

The markets themselves are a feast. Picture wooden chalets sending out clouds of steam and the air thick with scents of spiced wine, melted cheese, and roasted nuts. My nose always leads me to a **raclette stand** first: golden wheels of cheese bubbling under heat lamps, scraped onto bread or potatoes until the gooey richness drips down your fingers. It's decadent, messy, and utterly comforting.

Then there's **frites**, Belgian fries served in paper cones. Don't mistake these for the thin, pale versions you might know elsewhere—Belgian frites are double-fried for crisp perfection, fluffy inside with a satisfying crunch. Smother them in mayo or andalouse sauce (a tangy mix of mayo, ketchup, and spices) and you'll understand why locals defend their fry culture so passionately.

For meat lovers, the scent of **sausages sizzling on grills** is impossible to ignore. Juicy bratwurst or spicy merguez tucked into buns, topped with onions, are a market staple. And on colder nights, I crave **carbonnade flamande**—a slow-cooked beef stew made with Belgian beer, hearty and sweet-savory, served with bread to mop up every last drop.

Belgium's Sweet Tooth: Waffles, Speculoos & Chocolate

Belgium's reputation for sweets is richly deserved, and I'll confess: I've indulged shamelessly.

Waffles come in two main types. The **Brussels waffle** is light, crisp, rectangular, dusted simply with powdered sugar or perhaps topped with whipped cream and fruit. The **Liège waffle**, by contrast, is denser, chewier, with caramelized sugar pearls baked right in. I can never decide which I love more, so I always end up with both. Walking through the market with a warm waffle in hand feels like the essence of Belgian winter.

Then there's **speculoos**, spiced shortcrust biscuits often stamped with festive patterns. The flavor is cinnamon-ginger warmth wrapped up in crunch. They're delicious on their own, but even better as a spread—creamy, caramel-like, and utterly addictive on toast. I always bring jars home, though they rarely last long.

And of course, **chocolate**. Belgium's crown jewel. Every chocolatier takes pride in pralines, truffles, and bars that taste like edible jewels.

Imagine biting into a praline: a crisp shell that gives way to a silky hazelnut cream, or dark ganache that melts luxuriously on the tongue. In Bruges, I once stumbled upon a tiny shop where the chocolatier dusted truffles with cocoa powder in front of me—it felt like watching art being born.

Beer Culture: From Abbey Ales to Cozy Bars

Belgian beer isn't just a drink—it's a culture, a tradition, a kind of liquid storytelling. Each brew carries history, often tied to abbeys or family recipes passed down through generations.

I always recommend trying a **Trappist ale**, brewed by monks in monasteries. Chimay, Westmalle, and Orval are famous examples—rich, complex, with fruity, yeasty notes that unfold slowly. Pair one with a plate of cheese and you've got a meal fit for kings.

For something lighter, the crisp citrus zing of a **witbier (white beer)** is refreshing, even in winter. And then there are **lambics and gueuze**, sour beers brewed with wild yeasts unique to Belgium. They're an acquired taste, tart and funky, but unforgettable once you fall for them.

The experience is just as important as the beer. In Brussels, I love slipping into centuries-old bars with low ceilings, wooden beams, and candles flickering on tables. In Bruges, cafés by the canal glow warmly at night, inviting you to linger with a glass while snowflakes drift past the window.

Top Restaurants & Cafés for Every Traveler

Markets are wonderful, but sometimes you crave a sit-down meal or a cozy café. Luckily, both cities deliver in spades.

- **For a splurge:** In Brussels, fine-dining spots near the Sablon serve inventive takes on Belgian classics. In Bruges, Michelin-starred restaurants like De Karmeliet (when open) elevate local flavors into artful plates. Perfect for a romantic evening.
- **Mid-range gems:** Look for brasseries with hearty Belgian staples—moules-frites (mussels with fries), waterzooi (a creamy chicken or

fish stew), or stoemp (mashed potatoes with vegetables, often paired with sausage). These dishes are satisfying, flavorful, and easy on the wallet.

- **Cafés & tea rooms:** Belgium excels at cozy hideaways. In Bruges, I once ducked into a tearoom on a snowy afternoon and was served hot chocolate so rich it felt like liquid velvet, alongside a slice of apple tart. In Brussels, cafés near Sainte-Catherine offer steaming bowls of soup with crusty bread, perfect for market breaks.

Vegan, Vegetarian & Dietary Options

Belgian cuisine is traditionally rich, but I've noticed in recent years that vegan and vegetarian travelers are being embraced more warmly.

In Brussels, plant-based restaurants around the city center serve creative dishes that echo Belgian flavors—think vegan "stoofvlees" (stew) made with seitan, or dairy-free waffles topped with seasonal fruit. Bruges, though smaller, also has vegetarian cafés and bakeries. I've found cozy spots offering soups, grain bowls, and even vegan chocolates.

Gluten-free travelers will also find options. Many chocolatiers and bakers label their treats clearly, and some restaurants now offer gluten-free beer or bread upon request. The key, as always, is to ask—Belgians are generally friendly and happy to help accommodate.

To me, the food in Brussels and Bruges isn't just about eating—it's about experiencing Belgium in every sense. The crunch of a fry dipped in tangy sauce, the perfume of spiced wine rising in frosty air, the warmth of chocolate melting on your tongue, the clink of beer glasses raised in centuries-old bars. These tastes stay with you long after the trip ends.

When I think of Belgium's winter markets, I don't just see the lights—I taste them. I taste the caramelized edges of a Liège waffle, the malty sweetness of a Trappist ale, the cinnamon-ginger kiss of a speculoos biscuit. And that, more than anything, is what keeps me coming back: the joy of indulgence, shared with others in the glow of the season.

SHOPPING & SOUVENIRS

There's something about strolling through a winter market that turns even the most practical traveler into a wide-eyed shopper. I can tell you, I've gone to "just browse" more times than I can count and still ended up hauling home ornaments, scarves, and jars of mustard I never knew I needed. Brussels and Bruges are a gift-giver's dream—every stall feels like a tiny boutique set inside a snow globe. The trick is knowing where to find the treasures, how to spot the authentic Belgian gems, and how to avoid the "made in elsewhere" trinkets that sometimes sneak in. Let's dive into the festive world of shopping, where the scent of cinnamon candles meets the sparkle of Christmas baubles.

Best Stalls for Handcrafted Gifts

If there's one piece of advice I give to anyone wandering the markets, it's this: **follow your nose and your curiosity.** Some stalls call you in with the smell of beeswax, others with the soft glow of wool mittens stacked like candy. In Brussels' Winter Wonders, the stalls around Place Sainte-Catherine are a haven for handmade crafts. Think leather-bound journals, wooden toys carved with delicate detail, and scarves handwoven in Belgium's countryside.

In Bruges, Simon Stevinplein transforms into a shopper's paradise. I once stumbled across a stall selling hand-blown glass ornaments where the artist painted each one on the spot. Watching that process was like witnessing Christmas magic in real time. These markets reward those who linger. Take your time, chat with the stallholders, and don't be shy about asking where the products come from—they're usually proud to share their stories.

Spotting Authentic Belgian Products

Let's be honest—there are plenty of shiny things at winter markets that look tempting but aren't truly Belgian. So how do you spot the real deal? **Labels, location, and storytelling.** If a vendor lights up when explaining how their grandmother's recipe inspired their speculoos biscuits, you know you've struck gold.

Some of the most authentic Belgian treasures include:

- **Lace from Bruges**: Hand-made lace is delicate, intricate, and unmistakably authentic when you see the fine craftsmanship up close. Don't confuse it with machine-made imitations—it's worth investing in a real piece, even if it's small.
- **Belgian chocolate**: Of course, but look for smaller chocolatiers rather than mass-market brands. The flavors are richer, the artistry more personal, and the gift box feels like a story in itself.
- **Tin-glazed ceramics**: Often painted in festive blues and whites, these pieces are lovely souvenirs for the home.

Think of authenticity as buying a story, not just a product. Every time I pull out a hand-painted ornament from Bruges, I remember the frosty night I bought it, hot chocolate in one hand and mittened fingers fumbling cash in the other.

Christmas Ornaments, Candles & Keepsakes

Here's where the festive magic really comes alive. Even if you're not a big shopper,

ornaments and candles are irresistible.
They're small, packable, and loaded with memory. In Brussels, I found carved wooden ornaments shaped like miniature beer steins (only in Belgium, right?). In Bruges, a stall glittered with crystal snowflakes that caught the light from every angle.

Candles are another winter market staple. Beeswax, spiced orange, cinnamon, pine—you'll find scents that turn your suitcase into a holiday treasure chest. I always grab a couple because lighting one back home instantly transports me to those cobbled squares.

And then there are the keepsakes that don't necessarily shout "Christmas," but still carry the spirit. A wool hat knitted by hand, a quirky ceramic mug, or even a jar of artisanal mustard can hold as much festive cheer as a bauble. (Yes, mustard—Belgians take it seriously, and it makes for a deliciously unexpected gift!)

Ethical & Sustainable Shopping Choices

Now, before you run wild with your shopping bag, let me put on my thoughtful traveler hat for a moment. The holidays can sometimes encourage overbuying, but Brussels and Bruges offer plenty of ways to **shop consciously and sustainably.**

Look for artisans using local, natural materials—candles made from beeswax instead of paraffin, scarves woven from organic wool, or wooden toys carved from responsibly sourced wood. Many stalls now proudly display eco-friendly labels, and you'll often find artisans who make it part of their story.

I also recommend **buying fewer but better.** One carefully chosen piece of lace or a box of handmade chocolates will carry more joy than a bag of generic souvenirs. Plus, supporting small vendors directly means your euros go into keeping these traditions alive.

And don't forget—you can make your own shopping sustainable by bringing along a reusable bag or backpack. Market stalls will happily hand over your treasures wrapped in paper, but skipping excess plastic feels good (and leaves more room in your suitcase for waffles, trust me).

Final Word

Shopping in Brussels and Bruges during winter isn't just about buying things—it's about **experiencing the charm of craftsmanship, culture, and connection.** Every purchase becomes a little bookmark in your travel story. When I hang a lace star on my tree or unwrap a bar of dark praline chocolate, I'm not just remembering the item—I'm remembering the laughter of the stallholder, the glow of fairy lights, the hum of carols in the air.

So, shop with joy. Shop with curiosity. And maybe, like me, you'll discover that the real souvenirs aren't just the ones that fit in your bag, but the stories and memories that come with them.

EVENTS, FESTIVALS & ENTERTAINMENT

Winter in Belgium isn't just about sipping mulled wine and wandering through Christmas stalls—though, believe me, I'd happily do that every day. What really makes the season sparkle is the way **Brussels and Bruges come alive with concerts, parades, light festivals, and spontaneous bursts of performance.** I've found myself swept up in brass bands marching down cobbled streets, enchanted by choirs filling gothic cathedrals with music, and dazzled by light shows that make entire squares glow like enchanted theaters.

If shopping at the markets is the heart of winter in Belgium, then these events are the rhythm—the beat that keeps everything joyous and alive.

Concerts, Parades & Street Performances in Brussels

Brussels has a knack for blending high culture with street-level fun. One moment you'll be listening to a string quartet in a candlelit church, the next you'll be tapping your feet to a jazz band on a corner, surrounded by a crowd of strangers who suddenly feel like friends.

The **Winter Wonders festival** is the centerpiece, and it brings the city's streets to life with concerts and performances throughout December. The **Grand-Place**, already a wonder with its light and sound show, often hosts choirs that make the air feel positively electric. I still remember standing shoulder-to-shoulder with locals and travelers alike, hearing "Silent Night" sung in flawless harmony as the illuminated square twinkled around us. Goosebumps don't even begin to describe it.

You'll also catch **street parades**—colorful processions with drummers, dancers, and sometimes whimsical performers dressed as angels or toy soldiers. They march through the historic center, adding bursts of joy and surprise wherever they go. Keep your camera handy, but honestly, sometimes it's best just to soak it in with wide eyes and warm hands around a hot chocolate.

For a more intimate experience, Brussels' churches, like **Église Sainte-Catherine** or **Église des Riches Claires**, host holiday concerts where local musicians and choirs share their talents. If you're lucky enough to snag a seat, it's one of the most soul-stirring ways to experience the city's festive side.

Bruges Light Festival Highlights

Ah, Bruges—the little jewel box of Belgium that already feels like a fairy tale even without the holiday season. Add the **Bruges Light Festival**, and suddenly it's as though the entire town has been sprinkled with stardust.

The festival runs during the winter months and transforms landmarks, canals, and tucked-away courtyards into glowing works of art. Each year has a different theme, and artists from around the world are invited to design installations that tell stories through light. One year I wandered past a row of trees wrapped in glowing ribbons that pulsed like heartbeats, and another time I saw entire facades painted with projections that made the buildings look as though they were moving.

Walking through Bruges at night during the festival feels like being inside a dream. The canals shimmer with reflections, and every corner invites a gasp or a smile. Families with children, couples holding hands, groups of friends laughing with mulled wine in hand—you'll see them all, moving slowly through the illuminated paths.

And don't miss the **ice rink** at the Market Square, which sparkles like a centerpiece surrounded by glowing chalets. Even if you don't lace up your skates, watching the joyful chaos of people gliding (and sometimes wobbling) under the lights is entertainment in itself.

The beauty of Bruges' light displays is that they're not confined to one place. The festival encourages you to explore—down alleys, across bridges, along the water. Each discovery feels personal, as though the city prepared a surprise just for you.

How to Find & Book Special Events

Now, here's where my practical side kicks in. With so much happening, how do you make sure you don't miss out on the best events? A little planning goes a long way.

For **Brussels**, the Winter Wonders website is your best friend. They keep an updated calendar of performances, from the big parades to small concerts. Many of the street performances are free and don't require reservations, but for indoor concerts—especially in churches or theaters—you'll want to book tickets in advance. Popular events sell out quickly, so if you have your heart set on something like a choral concert in the Grand-Place area, grab your tickets early.

For **Bruges**, the Light Festival is open to everyone, but some events within the festival—like guided light tours or ticketed exhibitions—need advance booking. You can check Bruges' official tourism site or stop by the tourist office near Market Square when you arrive. I've also found that local hotels often have insider tips or even special packages that include event access.

And here's a little travel hack: **ask locals.** I can't tell you how many times I've learned about a smaller concert or quirky street performance just by chatting with a barista or a market vendor. Belgians are proud of their winter traditions and usually delighted to share what's happening that week.

Final Word

What makes the events and festivals in Brussels and Bruges so special isn't just the music, the lights, or the pageantry—it's the feeling of **collective joy.** You're not just a spectator, you're part of the celebration. Whether you're singing along with strangers in a candlelit square, gasping at light art along Bruges' canals, or clapping to the beat of a marching band, you become woven into the festive fabric of the city.

And honestly, those are the moments that stick with me far longer than anything I bought or ate. I carry them home like invisible souvenirs—the sound of bells echoing off stone walls, the shimmer of reflections dancing on water, the laughter of people gathered under the same winter sky.

So, if you ask me, don't just shop, sip, and stroll—make room for the concerts, the parades, the festivals. Let yourself get caught up in the magic. Because in Belgium, the winter markets are only the beginning of the show.

THE MARKET SURVIVAL GUIDE

Here's the truth: as magical as Brussels' Winter Wonders and Bruges' Winter Glow are, they can also be crowded, chilly, and a little overwhelming if you go in unprepared. I've learned this the hard way—squeezed shoulder-to-shoulder with strangers, juggling a cup of mulled wine and a dripping waffle, while my toes froze faster than my hot chocolate cooled. But don't worry, that's why I'm here. Think of this as your friendly insider's cheat sheet to surviving (and actually thriving) in the markets.

Beating the Crowds & Finding Quiet Moments

First things first: let's talk about crowds. These markets attract thousands daily, and if you're not strategic, you'll feel like a sardine in a festive tin.

Timing is everything. If you can, visit on weekday afternoons. That's when families and office workers are at school or work, leaving you room to breathe. Fridays and Saturdays after 6 p.m.? Those are prime-time crush hours—beautiful, but busy. If you want the sparkle of lights without the stampede, aim for a late Sunday evening stroll.

Here's one of my favorite hacks: **start at the edges.** In Brussels, most people pile straight into the Grand-Place and Sainte-Catherine zones. Instead, begin your wanderings at the outer markets (like Place de la Monnaie), and work inward. You'll catch the atmosphere while everyone else is cramming into the main square.

And don't forget Bruges. Because it's smaller, the crowds feel more concentrated. My trick? Duck into side streets or along the canals for a breather. Sometimes the best moments aren't in the heart of the crowd but in the quieter glow of a side-stall or a lantern-lit bridge.

Keeping Warm Outdoors

Now, let's get practical: staying warm. If you think you'll be fine with just a coat, think again. Belgian winters have a sneaky chill—it's damp, it seeps into your bones, and it doesn't care if you've layered up "just enough."

Here's my formula: **three layers, minimum.** A thermal base (yes, they're worth it), a cozy sweater, and a windproof coat. Add a scarf (bonus points if it doubles as a blanket), gloves (preferably touchscreen-friendly), and a hat that covers your ears. Forget fashion-first footwear—this is a boots-and-thick-socks kind of adventure.

And here's a little insider move: **keep hand warmers in your pockets.** Those tiny packets of magic can turn a long stroll from misery to merriment. If you don't want to carry them, duck into a café every hour or so for a warm-up—think of it as a cultural immersion disguised as a survival tactic.

Of course, don't underestimate the power of warm drinks. Mulled wine, hot chocolate, or even a steaming cup of Belgian soup can double as both sustenance and hand heaters. I once carried a hot cone of frites purely to thaw my fingers—it worked like a charm.

Safety in Busy Spaces & Crowd Awareness

Let's face it: festive crowds are joyful, but they can also be chaotic. While Brussels and Bruges are generally very safe, a little awareness goes a long way.

Pickpockets love distracted tourists. So, keep your wallet, phone, and passport secure—front pockets, zipped bags, or even under-coat money belts if you're extra cautious. Backpacks are fine, but don't stash valuables in the outer pockets unless you want to give them away.

Another tip? **Be spatially aware.** Markets are full of people stopping suddenly to snap photos (I've been guilty of this too). If you don't want to wear someone else's hot chocolate, move slowly and give yourself room. And when it's really packed, go with the flow instead of fighting against it—you'll save yourself the stress.

Families with kids should set up a "just in case" meeting spot. I've seen plenty of little ones wide-eyed in the crowd, and while it's usually just a momentary separation, having a backup plan helps everyone relax.

Finally, stay alert crossing roads between markets. Cars and bikes don't always share your festive glow, and Belgian cyclists especially take no prisoners.

Money-Saving Tips for Food & Gifts

Now let's talk about money. Winter markets can seduce your wallet faster than you can say "speculoos." A few smart moves can stretch your euros without dampening the fun.

First up: **eat strategically.** Sampling everything is tempting, but prices add up. I like to treat myself to one or two "splurge" items (like a gourmet waffle smothered in Belgian chocolate) and balance it out with heartier, cheaper bites like frites or sausage rolls. Portions are usually generous, so sharing with a friend means you get to try more without breaking the bank—or your belt.

For drinks, remember that mulled wine and hot chocolate often come with a **mug deposit system.** You'll pay a few extra euros upfront, which you get back when you return the mug. If you like the mug design, you can keep it as a souvenir—two birds, one stone.

When it comes to gifts, **set a budget before you dive in.** The glow of fairy lights makes everything look irresistible. To avoid impulse buying, I usually do one "scouting lap" to see what's on offer, then circle back for the must-haves.

And here's my secret weapon: **markets aren't your only shopping option.** Step into nearby local shops for chocolates, lace, and other Belgian specialties. They often sell the same quality (if not better) at more reasonable prices, and you'll avoid the tourist markup.

Final word

The markets are dazzling, yes—but they're also a little wild. The trick isn't just to survive them, but to **enjoy them without exhaustion, frostbite, or an empty wallet.** Go at the right time, bundle up properly, keep an eye on your belongings, and spend smart.

With these insider moves, you'll not only make it through the markets comfortably—you'll have the energy (and cash) left to soak in the concerts, explore side streets, and maybe even splurge on that box of artisanal chocolates you swore you didn't need.

So, take it from me: the markets aren't a sprint, they're a festive marathon. Pace yourself, play it smart, and you'll leave with more joy (and souvenirs) than you thought possible.

FAMILY &
KID-FRIENDLY TRAVEL

I know from experience that traveling with family can be both the most rewarding and the most demanding way to see the world. The laughter of your child ice-skating under fairy lights, or the wonder on their face at a glowing parade, can be the highlight of your trip. But I also understand the quieter realities—strollers bumping over cobblestones, little ones getting cold quicker than adults, teenagers rolling their eyes when they'd rather be glued to a screen.

That's why I want to reassure you: **Brussels and Bruges are wonderfully family-friendly in winter.** Yes, there will be moments when mittens go missing or hot chocolate spills down a scarf, but there will also be joy so pure it takes your breath away. And with a little preparation, you can tip the balance toward the magical side.

Activities for Children & Teenagers

The markets themselves are like giant playgrounds. In Brussels, the **ice rink at Place De Brouckère** is always a hit. Little ones can wobble around with the help of skating aids shaped like penguins, while older kids and teens zip around with big grins (or exaggerated groans if they fall). I've seen whole families laughing together on the ice—it's a memory-maker, even if your ankles protest the next day.

Santa's Grotto at Brussels' Winter Wonders is another crowd-pleaser. Meeting Santa, with twinkling lights and festive music in the background, is the kind of moment younger kids will talk about long after the trip.

In Bruges, the **Light Festival** adds an extra layer of enchantment. Children often respond with wide-eyed wonder to the glowing installations, while teens love the interactive art displays and photo opportunities (yes, even the too-cool-for-this crowd usually ends up snapping selfies).

And let's not forget the simple pleasures: rides on the old-fashioned carousels, tasting sweet waffles dusted in sugar, or wandering along the canals where swans glide like something out of a fairy tale.

Family-Friendly Dining & Cafés

Food is part of the fun, and Belgium makes it easy to keep kids happy at mealtimes. **Frites (fries)** are practically a national treasure—crispy, golden, and served with a variety of sauces. They're cheap, quick, and almost universally adored by children.

For sweet treats, waffles and hot chocolate will win over even the pickiest eaters. In fact, one of my favorite family memories in Bruges was watching a child's face light up at a waffle so big it barely fit on the plate.

When it comes to sit-down dining, look for **casual brasseries** and cafés near the markets. Many welcome children and have a relaxed atmosphere where families won't feel rushed. In Brussels, I've found that the area around Sainte-Catherine has plenty of cozy spots with hearty soups, pastas, and sandwiches. In Bruges, the smaller cafés near Markt Square are warm havens where families can thaw out together.

Tip: if you've got teenagers with adventurous taste buds, encourage them to try Belgian classics like carbonnade flamande (a beef stew cooked in beer). It's hearty, warming, and might just surprise them.

Tips for Visiting with Babies & Strollers

Now, let's talk about the littlest travelers. Brussels and Bruges are generally stroller-friendly, but the **cobblestones can be tricky.** A stroller with sturdy wheels will make your life much easier. Alternatively, many parents find a baby carrier or sling more practical for navigating the busiest parts of the markets.

For warmth, I recommend **layering up the baby** and bringing a cozy blanket or stroller cover to block the wind. Market nights can be damp, so waterproof covers are a good idea too.

Changing facilities are available in some cafés and larger public restrooms, but not always right where you need them. I suggest carrying a compact changing mat and being prepared for a little improvisation. The upside? Belgian café owners are generally kind and accommodating if you ask for help.

Finally, don't feel pressure to do everything. Families move at a different pace, and that's okay. Sometimes the best moments are the small ones—sharing hot chocolate on a bench, watching carolers together, or simply wandering without a set plan.

Final Word

Traveling with kids in Brussels and Bruges during the winter season is about embracing the magic while planning for the little bumps along the way. Yes, mittens will get lost. Yes, someone will get tired at exactly the wrong moment. But you'll also collect moments of pure joy—children squealing on the ice, teenagers secretly impressed by a glowing light display, parents catching each other's eye and smiling because it's all worth it.

So, bring the stroller, pack the snacks, and keep your sense of humor handy. These cities have a way of making the holidays feel like something out of a storybook, not just for kids, but for parents too.

COUPLES & ROMANCE

There's something about Belgium in winter that feels like it was designed for romance. Perhaps it's the way the cobblestone streets glisten after a light snowfall, or how the golden glow of street lamps reflects on medieval facades. Maybe it's the comforting ritual of wrapping cold hands around a shared cup of steaming hot chocolate, your breath mingling with the frosty air. Whatever it is, Brussels and Bruges have a way of slowing time, creating space for quiet moments where love feels as magical as the twinkling lights strung across the markets.

Most Romantic Spots in Brussels & Bruges

When I think of romance in Brussels, my mind immediately drifts to the **Grand-Place** at dusk. Standing arm in arm beneath the soaring Gothic towers, you'll be surrounded by a golden glow that feels both grand and intimate. It's the kind of place where you instinctively pull each other closer, soaking up the beauty that seems to belong only to you.

Another gem is the **Mont des Arts gardens**. Even in winter, the view over the city, with the spire of the Town Hall in the distance, feels cinematic. I like to linger there just before evening, when the sky turns deep shades of pink and indigo—a backdrop that makes even the simplest stroll feel like a page out of a love story.

And then, there's Bruges. Oh, Bruges. This city is like a living love letter. Walking along its canals is pure poetry. In the quiet of winter, when the day-trippers have gone, the stillness feels sacred. The **Minnewater, or "Lake of Love,"** lives up to its name. Standing on the bridge with your partner, gazing at the swans gliding across the water, it's impossible not to feel wrapped in a timeless romance.

At night, Bruges' canals shimmer under soft lights, and the little stone bridges seem to whisper secrets of lovers' past. Even a simple walk through the winding streets feels enchanting—you'll pass hidden courtyards, candlelit restaurants, and windows aglow with holiday warmth.

Proposal & Anniversary Ideas

If you're planning something unforgettable—like a proposal—Belgium provides endless inspiration. Imagine popping the question in front of the **Grand-Place light and sound show**, where the music swells and the buildings shimmer with festive colors. It's dramatic, dazzling, and guaranteed to leave you both breathless.

For something quieter and more intimate, the **Begijnhof in Bruges** offers a serene, almost spiritual backdrop. In winter, the peaceful courtyard dusted with frost feels private, like the world has hushed just for you. Kneeling down here, amid centuries-old walls and a sense of enduring history, adds a tender depth to the moment.

Anniversaries are equally special here. A private **canal boat ride in Bruges**, bundled up under blankets while the city glides by, feels like stepping into a dream. In Brussels, you could celebrate with a candlelit dinner in **Sablon**, the elegant neighborhood known for its chocolatiers and historic charm. End the night with a slow walk through the illuminated markets, hand in hand, letting the festive spirit linger.

Cozy Hotels, Restaurants & Experiences for Two

Choosing the right place to stay can make your romantic escape even more magical. In Brussels, I'd suggest looking near the **Sablon** or **Ixelles** districts. Boutique hotels here often come with plush interiors, fireplaces, and the kind of attentive service that makes you feel pampered. Some even have rooms with balconies overlooking the rooftops—a perfect spot to sip champagne together before heading out into the night.

In Bruges, romance is everywhere. Opt for a historic hotel along the canal, where you can watch the water glisten outside your window. Many offer four-poster beds, soft candlelight, and breakfast in bed—luxuries that make you want to linger indoors just as much as you want to explore outside.

When it comes to dining, I always lean toward intimate, tucked-away spots. In Brussels, a dinner at **Comme Chez Soi**, with its Michelin-starred menu and Art Nouveau setting, feels indulgent but oh so worth it for a special occasion. In Bruges, a cozy bistro near the Market Square, with flickering candles and hearty Flemish stew, is perfect for warming up after a chilly evening walk.

Don't forget the simple pleasures, too—sharing a warm waffle dusted with powdered sugar, sipping glühwein at the market, or sneaking into a café for hot chocolate so thick it feels like velvet. These little indulgences, enjoyed together, often become the memories you cherish most.

Finally, one of my favorite romantic rituals is to take a late-night stroll after the markets close. The streets quiet down, the crowds disappear, and the city feels like it belongs to just the two of you. Walking slowly, hands entwined, with only the crunch of footsteps on cobblestones and the glow of lanterns above—it's a moment of intimacy that no guidebook can fully capture.

Love, after all, is found in these small, tender moments. Brussels and Bruges, with their twinkling lights, medieval charm, and winter warmth, provide the perfect stage for those moments to unfold. Whether it's a grand proposal, a milestone anniversary, or simply a stolen kiss under the glow of Christmas lights, Belgium in winter whispers one thing clearly: romance is everywhere, if you pause to let it in.

PHOTOGRAPHY &
INSTAGRAM MOMENTS

Whenever I travel, my camera—or at least my phone—is like an extra limb. In Belgium during the winter, it's impossible not to feel like every corner begs to be framed, every cobblestone seems to whisper, "capture me." Brussels and Bruges in December aren't just destinations; they're living postcards, with colors, lights, and textures that seem designed for a perfect Instagram grid. Let me take you through how I've found the most breathtaking shots, and how you can catch them too.

Best Sunrise & Sunset Spots

If there's one thing I've learned, it's that the early bird photographer is always rewarded. In **Bruges**, sunrise over the canals is nothing short of magical. I once stood on **Rozenhoedkaai**, shivering slightly, watching the first light pour over the water like liquid gold. The medieval facades, mirrored in the still canal, looked as if they were glowing from within. Hardly anyone was around—just me, the swans, and a few bundled-up locals cycling past. For Instagram, these moments are priceless: the light is soft, the reflections perfect, and the mood pure fairy tale.

In **Brussels**, my go-to sunrise spot is the **Mont des Arts gardens**. From this little terrace, the view stretches all the way to the Town Hall spire. At sunrise, the city feels hushed, the rooftops bathed in a rosy glow. It's not just a photo—it's a mood. And if you're more of a sunset person, **Bruges' Belfry tower** rewards you with sweeping golden views across the Market Square, while in Brussels, **Parc du Cinquantenaire** frames the sky behind its grand archway in dramatic, fiery hues.

Capturing the Markets at Night

Now, let's talk about the magic hour—the moment the Christmas markets really come alive. I've found that **blue hour** (that dreamy twilight just after sunset) is the sweet spot. The sky still holds a hint of color, while the market lights sparkle like stars. In Brussels' **Grand-Place**, the towering Christmas tree surrounded by golden guild houses looks even more striking against the deepening sky. I like to stand back a little and capture the whole square, with people blurred in motion, giving the shot both scale and energy.

In Bruges, I recommend heading to **Simon Stevinplein** once the stalls are glowing. The cozy scale of the market makes for intimate, detail-rich shots—candles flickering, ornaments twinkling, cups of mulled wine steaming in the cold. Zoom in on the little things: a hand holding a waffle dusted with sugar, a child staring wide-eyed at a toy stall, the soft reflections of lights in a puddle. These are the photos that tell the story of the moment, not just the place.

And don't be afraid to experiment. Try a long exposure on your phone (yes, even most phones can handle it now) to capture the skating rink in Brussels with streaks of movement—like ribbons of light gliding across the ice.

Photo Secrets Only Locals Know

Here's the fun part—the little photography secrets that not everyone stumbles upon. In Bruges, slip away from the crowds and head to the **Begijnhof**. In winter, its quiet courtyard and whitewashed houses look like a painting. If snow has fallen, it's pure minimalism—a perfect frame of peace and symmetry.

In Brussels, I once ducked into a narrow side street near the **Galeries Royales Saint-Hubert**, only to find a hidden angle where the arcade's glass roof caught the reflection of holiday lights outside. Hardly anyone passes there, which makes it even better—you'll feel like you've uncovered a secret backdrop for your photo story.

For a bit of whimsy, I also like to frame Belgium's famous treats in the shot. A hot cone of frites held up with the market behind it, or a perfectly decorated Belgian chocolate truffle on a napkin by the canals—it gives your photo both flavor and personality. Instagram isn't just about pretty scenery; it's about the small moments that make your trip uniquely yours.

When I look back at my Belgium photos, I don't just see places—I feel the warmth of glühwein in my hands, the thrill of a first snowfall, the sparkle of laughter under fairy lights. That's what the best pictures do: they don't just freeze time, they carry the atmosphere forward. So whether you're after likes, memories, or both, remember this—Belgium in winter isn't just photogenic, it's cinematic. You're not just taking pictures; you're capturing magic.

ACCESSIBILITY & SENIOR-FRIENDLY TRAVEL

Whenever I talk about traveling to Belgium in the winter, one of the things I feel most strongly about is this: these magical cities should be open to everyone. Whether you're exploring with a wheelchair, navigating with a cane, or simply planning your adventure with comfort in mind as a senior traveler, Brussels and Bruges have more resources and adaptations than many realize. My goal here is to share what I've learned so you can feel not only prepared but also confident that this trip is meant for you, too.

Wheelchair Access & Mobility Tips

I've walked the cobblestones of Bruges and Brussels countless times, and I know firsthand they can look intimidating. But with a bit of planning, they don't have to be a barrier. Both cities have been steadily improving accessibility—ramps, curb cuts, and accessible entrances are more common than you might expect in historic areas.

In **Brussels**, the **Grand-Place** has level access on most sides, making it possible to roll into the heart of the market without too much trouble. Many of the stalls and food stands are open-front, which means browsing from wheelchair height is doable. Public transportation is also becoming more inclusive: metro lines and buses offer low-floor access and designated seating. I always advise checking the **STIB/MIVB website** for updated info on which stations are most wheelchair-friendly.

Bruges, being smaller and more medieval, does present challenges with its uneven cobblestones. But the main squares, like the **Markt** and **Simon Stevinplein**, are relatively smooth and accessible. Wheelchair users will find it helpful to stick to the wider streets and canalside promenades, where paving is more even. If you're worried about fatigue, I've seen many travelers take advantage of **mobility scooter rentals**—a wonderful option if you want independence without overexertion.

My tip? Don't be shy about asking locals or market staff for help—they're used to it, and in my experience, they respond with warmth and respect.

Senior Travel Recommendations

For senior travelers, winter markets can be both exhilarating and tiring. The good news is, Belgium is very accommodating if you pace yourself. In Brussels, I always recommend starting at the **Mont des Arts gardens**, where the incline is gentle and benches are plentiful—perfect for resting between strolls. Once you're at the Winter Wonders market, you'll find plenty of cozy cafés where you can warm up with hot chocolate or mulled wine. These breaks aren't just practical; they're part of the joy.

In Bruges, the compact size of the city is actually an advantage for seniors. You don't need to walk far to see a lot. A **horse-drawn carriage ride** through the old streets can be a magical, restful way to take in the scenery. Canal boat rides are another senior-friendly option; the boarding areas usually have staff to assist, and once seated, the pace is gentle and relaxing.

I've often suggested staying near the squares themselves—like around **Markt in Bruges** or close to the **Grand-Place in Brussels**—so that walking distances to the markets are short. And if stairs are a concern, many boutique hotels and modern accommodations do offer elevators, though it's always best to confirm before booking.

Services & Resources for Special Needs Travelers

What I find reassuring is how many support services exist in Belgium for travelers with special needs. **Tourist information centers** in both cities provide accessibility guides, highlighting which attractions, routes, and facilities are best equipped. In Brussels, I've seen brochures specifically designed for mobility-impaired visitors, which can save a lot of guesswork.

Medical services are also close at hand. Pharmacies are easy to spot (look for the green cross signs), and most staff speak English well enough to assist. For more serious concerns, hospitals in both Brussels and Bruges are modern, accessible, and welcoming to international visitors.

Another underappreciated resource? **Guided tours tailored for accessibility.** Some operators offer private walking tours designed for wheelchair users or slower-paced groups. These guides know exactly which routes are smoother, where accessible toilets are located, and how to avoid unnecessary strain. I can't recommend them enough if you want peace of mind.

For travelers who need additional support, Belgium also has **mobility assistance at train stations and airports**. If you book in advance, staff can help with boarding, luggage, and transfers—something that makes the journey much smoother.

When I think about accessibility and senior-friendly travel, I picture the glowing faces of travelers I've met—people who thought a trip like this might not be possible, only to discover it was not only doable but delightful. Yes, there may be cobblestones, chilly evenings, and the occasional busy crowd. But with thoughtful planning and the right resources, the Brussels and Bruges winter markets are as open to you as to anyone else.

You deserve to sip mulled wine under the twinkling lights, glide past medieval facades on a canal boat, or simply sit by the fire in a cozy café watching the world go by. These experiences aren't just for the young or the fast-paced; they're for everyone. And I promise, once you're there, you'll feel that magic—steady, inclusive, and entirely yours.

PRACTICAL ESSENTIALS

One of the things I've learned after years of traveling is that the magic of a place—its lights, its flavors, its festive atmosphere—always shines brighter when the practical details are under control. That's why I like to sit down before every trip and run through the basics: money, safety, connectivity, and health. These may not be the most glamorous parts of travel, but they're what give you peace of mind so you can focus on enjoying every waffle, light show, and snow-dusted square.

Budgeting & Daily Costs

When it comes to Brussels and Bruges in winter, I find costs to be moderate by Western European standards—less expensive than Paris, but not as cheap as some Eastern European destinations. A comfortable daily budget, in my experience, runs something like this:

- **Budget travelers** (hostels, street food, public transport): €60–€90 per day
- **Mid-range travelers** (3-star hotels, sit-down meals, occasional taxi): €120–€180 per day

- **Luxury travelers** (4–5-star hotels, fine dining, guided tours): €250+ per day

At the markets themselves, I usually allow about **€20–€30** for food and drinks if I'm grazing on mulled wine, waffles, and small bites. Handmade gifts and crafts can range from **€10 for ornaments** to **€100+ for artisanal lace or specialty chocolates**. My advice? Carry a "market fund" in mind, so you know how much you're comfortable spending each day. It's easy to get caught up in the festive spirit and overspend without realizing it.

Currency, Payments & Tipping

Belgium uses the **euro (€)**, and I've found that both Brussels and Bruges are very card-friendly. Most market stalls accept credit and debit cards, and contactless payments are common. Still, I always keep some cash on hand—about €20–€40 in small bills—for little purchases like carousel rides for kids or a cone of fries from a street vendor.

As for tipping, Belgium doesn't operate on the same system as the U.S. Service charges are included in restaurant bills. That said, if I've had particularly warm service, I like to round up a euro or two, or leave 5–10% at a sit-down restaurant. In cafés or bars, rounding up to the nearest euro is perfectly fine. For taxis, I typically round up to the next euro as well.

Safety, Health & Emergency Numbers

Both Brussels and Bruges feel very safe to me, even at night when the markets are glowing with activity. That said, like any busy city, pickpockets can appear in crowded areas. I always carry my wallet and phone in a zippered pocket or crossbody bag. A simple precaution, but it saves worry.

Health-wise, Belgium's medical system is excellent. Pharmacies are everywhere (look for the green cross signs), and pharmacists are knowledgeable—they can often help with minor issues without needing a doctor's visit. If you ever do need urgent help, the main **emergency number in Belgium is 112**, which covers police, fire, and ambulance.

I also keep a mental note of Brussels' major hospitals, such as **Cliniques Universitaires Saint-Luc**, and Bruges' **AZ Sint-Jan Hospital**, just in case. If you're traveling with kids, elderly family members, or anyone with a condition that might require extra care, it's worth writing these down before your trip.

Essential Apps, SIM Cards & Connectivity

Staying connected in Belgium is simple. Free Wi-Fi is available in many hotels, restaurants, and even public spaces. But I prefer to have my own mobile data—it makes navigating the markets and checking train times stress-free.

You can buy a local **SIM card** at Brussels Airport or in the city at shops like Proximus, Orange, or BASE. Expect to pay around €15–€25 for a starter pack with several gigabytes of data. If you'd rather not swap out your SIM, **eSIM options** (like Airalo) work perfectly well across Belgium.

As for apps, a few I always recommend:

- **Google Maps** (obvious, but essential for walking routes and public transport directions).
- **STIB/MIVB app** for Brussels transport schedules.

- **NMBS/SNCB app** for national trains (especially handy for Brussels ↔ Bruges day trips).
- **Too Good To Go** if you're open to discounted food from local restaurants and bakeries—great for budget travelers.
- **Google Translate** (though English is widely spoken, it helps for menus or signs in Dutch/French).

When I think about practical essentials, I don't see them as boring checkboxes—I see them as the foundation for freedom. If you know your budget, have your cash and cards sorted, feel safe with emergency numbers in your pocket, and have data on your phone, the rest of the trip feels lighter. You're no longer worrying about "what ifs"; you're just walking through markets, sipping cocoa, and letting the magic of Belgium in winter unfold around you.

That's the whole point of this chapter: not to overload you with details, but to reassure you. With a few calm, clear steps, you'll have everything under control—so when the music starts playing in the Grand-Place or the candles glow on Bruges' canals, you're fully present, ready to enjoy every second.

ITINERARIES FOR EVERY TRAVELER

When I first began exploring Christmas markets across Belgium, I quickly realized that no two travelers arrive with the same amount of time, energy, or focus. Some people come for a magical one-day escape, others carve out a weekend, and still others want to linger for a week, soaking in every sparkle and flavor. That's why I've structured these itineraries like personal journeys—stories that you can slip into, hour by hour, as though you're walking alongside me. Each one is flexible, but together they'll help you capture the heart of Belgium's winter magic, no matter how long you stay.

One-Day Market Dash: Bruges or Brussels

If you only have a single day, I suggest choosing either **Bruges or Brussels**. Both cities deliver that quintessential Christmas market magic, but they offer it in different flavors.

Morning in Bruges: Imagine starting the day in Bruges, arriving as the town square slowly comes alive under strings of lights. I'd take you straight to the **Markt**, where the soaring Belfry looks down over stalls brimming with ornaments and chocolate. A hot waffle in hand, you'll wander cobblestone lanes lined with garlands.

Or Morning in Brussels: If Brussels is your pick, you'll begin in **Grand-Place**, which feels like a living snow globe. The gilded facades sparkle in daylight and even more under the evening light show. Start with a slow stroll through the **Winter Wonders Market**, picking up a steaming cup of mulled wine.

Afternoon: By midday, stop for a cozy Belgian lunch—think **stoofvlees** (beef stew) with frites. In Bruges, maybe you rent a bike to glide past canals fringed with frosted trees. In Brussels, you could duck into **Galeries Royales Saint-Hubert**, where chocolate shops tempt you with pralines wrapped like jewels.

Evening: As the day closes, you'll want to circle back to the market stalls as the lights flicker on. The atmosphere transforms—carousels spin, choirs sing, and the scent of spiced cookies fills the air. One day might not be enough, but it will feel like a pocket of enchantment tucked into your travels.

Two-Day Brussels Focus with a Market Glow

If I had two days in Brussels, I'd sink more deeply into the city's rhythms.

Day One: Arrive in the morning and spend time in **Grand-Place**, letting the golden façades welcome you. Visit **Winter Wonders**, which stretches from Bourse to Place Sainte-Catherine, alive with over 200 stalls. I'd take you ice skating under the Ferris wheel's glow before we pause for waffles dusted with powdered sugar.

That evening, you'd join me for dinner at a traditional brasserie—maybe **Chez Léon** for mussels—and then we'd circle back to Grand-Place for the **light and sound show**, one of the most stirring holiday experiences you can imagine.

Day Two: On the second day, we'd explore the museums and quieter corners—**Magritte Museum** for surrealist wonder, or **Musée des Instruments de Musique** with its panoramic rooftop café. By late afternoon, we'd head back toward the markets to catch any stalls we missed. I'd encourage you to buy a small keepsake here, something that carries the scent of cinnamon or the glow of woodcraft home with you.

Four-Day Twin-City Experience

For those with four days, nothing beats pairing **Brussels and Bruges**. It's like tasting two variations of the same Christmas carol—each city has its own melody.

Days One & Two: Brussels

I'd guide you much as I described earlier—soaking in Grand-Place, tasting chocolate, riding the Ferris wheel, and savoring brasserie meals. Take your time, because Brussels' markets are vast, and each turn reveals a new surprise: puppet shows, choirs, or even little rides for children.

Day Three: Travel to Bruges

The train ride to Bruges takes about an hour, and I promise you it feels like gliding into a fairy tale. Bruges is smaller and more intimate, and its canals shimmer with reflections of lights. The **Ice Sculpture Festival** often runs in winter and is worth a peek.

Day Four: Bruges Markets & Farewell

Spend your last day wandering between the Markt and Simon Stevinplein, picking up lace, chocolates, and handcrafted ornaments. In the evening, warm your hands around a cup of glühwein before heading back—your suitcase a little fuller, your heart completely so.

One-Week Immersive Winter Escape

If you can give yourself a week, this is where Belgium truly reveals its depth.

Days One–Two: Brussels

I'd begin with Brussels, just as before—soaking up Winter Wonders and diving into the museums. Give yourself time to sit in a café and watch locals bundled in scarves stroll by. The rhythm here feels cosmopolitan, but still cozy.

Days Three–Four: Bruges

Then, two days in Bruges. Beyond the markets, wander its quieter lanes. Take a canal cruise if weather allows, or climb the Belfry for sweeping views over rooftops dusted with snow. I always find that Bruges slows my pace, urging me to savor.

Days Five–Six: Ghent

From Bruges, hop over to **Ghent**, a city that glows with creativity and Gothic charm. Its Christmas market is lively yet less crowded. Wander Graslei, with its medieval guild houses reflected in the river, and visit **St. Bavo's Cathedral** for the Van Eyck altarpiece. Ghent feels both vibrant and intimate—perfect for balancing out Bruges' fairy tale with something more lived-in.

Day Seven: Leuven or Antwerp

Finally, choose between Leuven or Antwerp for your last day. Leuven charms with its university-town vibrancy and smaller markets. Antwerp dazzles with its Cathedral of Our Lady, fashion boutiques, and a market that spreads from Groenplaats to Steenplein. Either way, you'll leave Belgium with the sense that you've tasted its many holiday moods.

Final Word

Each of these itineraries is more than just a checklist—it's a journey, a living memory waiting to be made. Whether you're here for a day or a week, I encourage you to let yourself wander a little, pause often, and let the glow of the markets pull you in. Because in Belgium, the magic isn't only in the stalls or lights—it's in the way you feel when you're standing there, wrapped in warmth, with winter unfolding all around you.

CONCLUSION

As I sit and reflect on my time wandering through Belgium's Christmas markets, I realize that the memories I carry feel like treasures themselves. The glow of the lights, the warmth of mulled wine in my hands, and the simple joy of watching strangers laugh together under the winter sky—these are moments that stay with me long after the stalls have closed and the snow has melted away.

Travel, especially in winter, has a way of slowing us down. It pulls us into the present, urging us to savor not just the sights, but the scents, sounds, and emotions that surround us. That's why, as you prepare to close this chapter of your journey, I want to leave you not only with guidance, but also with a spark of inspiration—something to carry home with you, to brighten the days that follow.

Last-Minute Souvenir Ideas

Before you board your train, plane, or car home, take a moment for one final wander through the markets. I always find that some of the most meaningful souvenirs are the ones picked up at the very last minute—when I'm no longer rushing, but simply open to whatever feels right.

Perhaps it's a hand-carved wooden ornament that will hang on your tree for years, carrying with it the memory of Belgium's glowing squares. Maybe it's a box of pralines from a chocolatier whose craft feels like edible art. Or it might be something simple—a pair of wool mittens knitted with care, a jar of spiced jam, or even a small candle whose scent will take you back in an instant.

For me, these souvenirs are more than objects; they are anchors. Each time I light that candle or unwrap a chocolate, I'm reminded not only of the beauty of Belgium's markets but also of how alive I felt while exploring them.

Reflections on Winter in Belgium

Winter in Belgium is more than a season—it's an atmosphere, a way of being. It's standing in **Grand-Place** in Brussels, wrapped in the collective awe of a crowd as the light show begins. It's strolling along the canals in Bruges, where the reflections of lanterns shimmer on the water like strokes of gold. It's tasting your first warm waffle after a long walk through frosty streets, and realizing that happiness can be as simple as that.

What struck me most was not just the beauty of the markets, but the sense of connection they create. Strangers stand shoulder to shoulder, sharing food, laughter, and music. Children press their noses to toy stalls, while grandparents linger over mulled wine, recalling markets they visited decades before. In those moments, the barriers of language, culture, and background seem to soften. We're all just people, gathered together to celebrate light in the darkest season.

For me, that's the real gift of traveling to Belgium in winter. It's not only about what I saw, but about how I felt—grounded, joyful, and part of something larger than myself.

Inspiring Your Next Seasonal Journey

As you close this guide, I hope you feel a sense of both contentment and anticipation. The beauty of travel is that it never really ends; each journey plants the seed for the next. Maybe your time in Belgium will inspire you to seek out other Christmas markets across Europe—Vienna, Salzburg, or Prague. Or perhaps you'll decide to return here, revisiting familiar squares with new eyes, bringing friends or family along to share in the magic.

I've often found that the best journeys are the ones that leave me with more questions than answers. Where else can I find that same warmth, that same sparkle? What new traditions are waiting for me to discover? The beauty of winter travel is that every city offers its own melody, its own way of wrapping the cold season in celebration.

And here's something I carry with me every time I return home: the understanding that the magic of the markets doesn't have to stay behind. It lives on in the way I light candles on a dark evening, share a hearty meal with loved ones, or pause to admire the beauty of small, ordinary things.

A Final Word

If there's one message I want you to take away, it's this: travel is not just about places, it's about feelings. Belgium's Christmas markets may be temporary, but the joy they create is lasting. Let yourself carry that light with you—into your home, your traditions, and your dreams of journeys yet to come.

So as you pack your souvenirs and close your suitcase, remember this: the markets may fade with the season, but the magic you felt—the laughter, the warmth, the wonder—is yours to keep. And when the next winter arrives, who knows? Maybe you'll find yourself standing once again beneath strings of twinkling lights, ready to begin the story all over again.

Printed in Dunstable, United Kingdom